How to Mess Up Your Life!

One Lousy Day at a Time

Darrin Zeer

Conari Press

Thanks to C. S. Lewis for
The Screwtape Letters

First published in 2006 by Conari Press,
an imprint of Red Wheel/Weiser, LLC
With offices at:
500 Third Street, Suite 230
San Francisco, CA 94107
www.redwheelweiser.com

Library of Congress Cataloging-in-Publication Data available upon request
ISBN-10: 1-57324-279-9
ISBN-13: 978-1-57324-279-0

Cover and interior design by TG Design
Typeset in triplex, and Stamp Gothic
Cover illustration by Jonathan Evans © Getty Images

Printed in Canada
TCP
10 9 8 7 6 5 4 3 2 1

Listen Up!

Introduction vii

Part 1 How to Get Dumped! 1

Part 2 How to Get Fired! 27

Part 3 How to Get Depressed! 41

Part 4 How to Get Angry! 53

Part 5 How to Get Stressed! 67

Happily Ever After! 85

Acknowledgments 86

About the Author 87

To make your reading experience more entertaining and effective, please read this book aloud in a high, whiney voice! However, I do not recommend reading it all in one sitting. Take it in small doses.

O.K., all you failures
Listen Up!

You can stop wondering...

Why you're always in such
a bad mood!

Why life can be so overwhelming!

Why you wake up in the morning
feeling bummed out!

Why your work mostly sucks!

And why your relationships always end up
in the dumps!

Don't blame yourself for being
so grumpy!

After all, you are only human!

Life sucks and shit happens (a lot)!

We all have our own special tips and tricks on how to mess up our lives. From generation to generation we have learned the important tools on how to ruin our own lives and the lives of those around us. Each of us has become quite proficient at messing things up! Is that not true?

In this book

I will in detail instruct you how to . . .

get dumped quickly and effectively

get fired whenever you want

get depressed all of the time

get angry in an instant and

get stressed all day long!

With determination and a losing attitude, you will become the least that you can be!

Words of Wisdom Through the Ages!

Just remember:

The glass is half empty!

The early bird catches your worm!

Put off until tomorrow what you
can do today!

Live each day as if it already were your last!

Your life is what others make of it!

There are hardly any fish in the sea!

You lose some, you lose some!

You are all that matters!

No matter where you go, you aren't there!

Don't forgive and don't ever forget!

Part 1

How to
Get Dumped!

The goal of "How to Get Dumped!" is to learn how to create an environment where the person you are married to or going out with can

hardly stand you!

Develop a relationship built on distrust, meanness, and a bitter feeling of dislike.

Crummy Couple's Therapy
Lesson #1

Lousy Listening Skills!

*"Listening is like the sound of one hand clapping.
Better to interrupt!"*

When your partner talks with you, just pretend to listen.

If you have been with each other for a long time, you probably have heard it all before.

Keep repeating the words, "Oh really . . . yes . . . oh really . . . uh-huh!"

Alternate your tone of voice depending on your partner's mood. Use a tragic tone if they are feeling up and an enthusiastic voice when they are feeling down.

While your partner talks, that is a good time to think about what you want to say! When you are ready to speak, simply interrupt and share your thoughts. That way you won't forget what you want to say. It doesn't matter if your wise words are completely unrelated to the current conversation.

Follow your own conversational flow!

When speaking, try to position your self so you can see the television just over your partner's shoulder.

Crummy Couple's Therapy
Lesson #2

Share Every Thought!

"Words can be like raindrops in a heavy downpour!"

The moment your partner gets home from work is the best time to talk to them in detail.

Give them an exact account of how your day went.

You want to share everything!

Talk loud and fast to maximize the amount of information you can unload on your partner.

If your partner tries to escape, corner them!

If they walk away, raise your voice so they can still hear you throughout the house.

When your partner is away, call them and leave very long, drawn-out messages. Quickly blurt out the most important details—for example, a phone number. That way your partner will have to listen to the sweet sound of your voice several times to correctly gather your information.

True friends stab you in the front.
OSCAR WILDE

```
Dear Doctor Dread,
I had a date with a hot babe last
night and she talked nonstop. How
can I tell her politely to shut up?
                    Yours truly,
            Motor Mouth Misery

Dear Motor Mouth Misery,
Good news, you don't have to tell
her a thing—just wear earplugs when
you are with her. As her lips move,
simply nod your head up and down.
If she looks at you for a response,
just say, "Yes, that's great!"
```

Crummy Couple's Therapy Lesson #3

The Blame Game!

"The secret to successful conflict is to blame the other!"

Always tell your partner when they make mistakes. It's an important part of having a relationship. You can dump your tension on your partner as a way to manage the frustration in your own life.

The name of the game is to prove that your partner is always wrong and you are always right.

At times you may even need to make up stuff to support your case.

Make your partner feel guilty.

The best defense is a good offense. Do everything possible to make them understand that they are the cause of your unhappiness.

Repeat lines like, "It's your fault" or "Don't you see what you have done to me?"

The "Blame Game" is a way that both of you can sharpen your argumentation skills.

Take notice when you score a "hit" and remember to use that same line in future arguments.

Crummy Couple's Therapy Lesson #4

Negative Relationship Affirmations!

"It's usually best to think the worst!"

Choose your favorite negative affirmations or make a special one up for yourself. It will help remind you of how miserable your relationship is.

(Please repeat throughout the day. Especially if you are getting along with your partner.)

I hate you! I hate you! I hate you! I hate you! You are not the one! You are not the one! You are not the one! Our relationship sucks! Our relationship sucks! Our relationship sucks! It's your fault! It's your fault! It's your fault! I can't trust you! I can't trust you! I can't trust you! You revolt me!!!!

In time you will find yourself simply repeating these affirmations without having to think about it.

```
Dear Doctor Dread,
I met a guy for dinner! He seems
so nice. He shares his feelings
openly and treated me like a lady.
Do you think I can trust him?
                    Yours truly,
                    Perfect Performer

Dear Perfect Performer,
Don't trust him! Declare yourself
celibate and get a pet. Dogs are
wonderful listeners.
```

Lousy Lover Tip #1

Kill The Chemistry!

"Falling in love is like falling on your face!"

Don't let yourself get dangerously lost in his/her dreamy eyes.

If you start to feel those telltale feelings of attraction, here are some tips to suppress your desires.

Avoid spending too much time with your date's "good side."

Try and avoid physical contact.

On romantic walks, keep a brisk pace.

Skip the romance and introduce your prospective partner to the "real you"! Tell your date about all your relationships that went sour.

Ask pointed questions about your date's history.

This will keep them off balance and unable to relax.

Find out why they got dumped in the past.

Focus on his/her odd quirks.

Don't let the chemistry get the better of you!

Lousy Lover Tip #2

Tantric Tantrum!

"Live for yourself; forget about others!"

Being a lousy lover takes skill!

Avoid gentle touches and sweet kisses. It exposes your weak side and makes you vulnerable.

If things get deep and meaningful, strike up a superficial conversation.

Focus on your own pleasure when you are making out with your partner.

During foreplay, aim about three inches away from your partner's erogenous zones.

After sex, it's best not to cuddle.

Leave immediately after climaxing.

If you begin to entertain romantic thoughts about your partner, just remind yourself that this person will soon be inflicting a lot of emotional pain upon you.

The majority of husbands remind me of an orangutan trying to play the violin.

HONORÉ DE BALZAC

Lousy Lover Tip #3

Spooning Phobia!

"You were born alone, you will die alone, so be alone!"

Spooning will make you feel claustrophobic! It should be avoided because it will leave you feeling too intimate with your partner.

Always fight for your own personal space; the first place to claim your territory is in bed.

While sleeping, kick your feet and throw your arms around in a frantic manner.

Use your elbows as a weapon to keep your bedmate at a distance.

Always position the front of your body away from your partner.

If your bedmate sneaks up while you are asleep and tries to spoon, just slide forward and push your arms back.

While your partner is sleeping, try pushing them out of bed.

A good marriage would be between a blind wife and a deaf husband.

MICHEL DE MONTAIGNE

Dear Doctor Dread,
My lover snores like a grizzly
bear! We have tried everything to
keep him quiet but nothing works.
He is a fabulous lover but the
snoring is deafening. Should I
keep him or dump him?

Yours truly,
Almost Deaf

Dear Almost Deaf,
In the future, the moment your
lovemaking is finished, ask your
partner to sleep on the couch or
go home. Problem solved!

Dirty Talk!

Share with your lover some of these phrases to help cool things off under the sheets!

"You're not doing it right!"

"I don't like that!"

"Ouch! That hurts!"

"Don't touch me like that!"

"That tickles!"

"Not like that!"

"Not yet!"

"I'm not ready!"

"What are you doing?"

Disastrous Dating Game #1

You are the Center of the Universe!

"It's your world; we just live in it!"

Dating is the most fun when the focus is on you. Enjoy the sound of your own voice— listen to yourself talk for hours.

Share the special gifts that you possess.

Dazzle them with your superior intellect.

Share in-depth your heroic accomplishments.

Take your listeners on an extended journey into the tedious details of your life story.

Disastrous Dating Game #2

Bad Body Language!

"Kill a relationship before it kills you!"

Make sure your date doesn't feel you are attracted to her/him.

While sitting at a restaurant, wrap your arms and legs tightly together at all times.

Avoid eye contact!

If your date tries to look at you, just dart your eyes around and swing your head in the opposite direction.

Sit halfway on your seat and halfway off so you are ready for a quick exit in case the date begins to bomb.

Dear Doctor Dread,
I want to leave my girlfriend
without hurting her feelings.
What should I do?

> Yours truly,
> Mr. Nice

Dear Mr. Nice,
Make sure you don't have any of
your stuff at her place and that
she doesn't have a key to your
place. When you are ready, stop
calling her and don't return her
calls. She will get the message
eventually. Don't practice this
technique if you want to go out
with any of her girlfriends. It
will backfire!

Terrible Pickup Lines!!!

What's your sign?

I can see you're attracted to me.

I can see your aura!

Do you have genital herpes?

Are you an easy lay?

What names should we give our kids?

Would you like to meet my parents?

Want to have group sex with some of
my buddies?

Is that you who smells?

Disastrous Dating Game #3

Better Late or Never!

"If you desire a pretty nurse, you must be patient!"

Always arrive between 15 minutes to one hour after your arranged meeting time, especially if it is a first date!

Catch up on your errands while your date waits for your arrival—this way you know you will have a table waiting for you when you finally do get there.

Try to avoid letting her/him know you are behind schedule in order to neutralize his/her desire to forgive you when you finally arrive.

Always play hard-to-get.

Classified Ads!

Woman Seeking Man
I feel bitter and lonely and want someone to cling onto. Are you that special someone I can blame for my misery? I am a neurotic clean-freak and you are my nightmare in shining armor. Miserable single waits impatiently for your call!

Man Seeking Woman
I am a womanizer who likes cheap one-night stands. How would you like to be humiliated and then dumped by me? I am a slob and proud of it! Will you be my mommy and take care of me? Unemployed single still living with parents, looking for someone to do his dirty laundry.

Disastrous Dating Game #4

Soul Mate Search

"Searching for the perfect mate can bring you perfect misery!"

Dedicate yourself to a lifelong search for your soul mate.

Set impossibly high standards for your perfect partner.

Rejoice in the misery of the endless search for that special someone.

If you do find a good match, then quickly judge them for not being perfect.

If your potential mate exhibits a flaw, immediately start your soul mate search all over again.

Horrible Household Rule #1

Embrace Your Inner Slob!

"Cleanliness can't exist without messiness!"

Let the dishes pile up for your partner to clean.

If they give you attitude, remind them how hard you work and how much you give every day.

Hold on to the conviction that doing the dishes is really just a small token of the gratitude your partner should be showing you.

Leave old food in the fridge long past its expiration date. The stench will be your silent act of kitchen anarchy!

Leave your possessions around the house in a random manner—it is a form of artistic expression.

Create piles as a declaration of your independence.

Teach your partner how to love you unconditionally!

Dear Doctor Dread,
My husband is an absolute slob. All he does is watch television. He never misses a single football game. How can I change him?

Yours truly,
Sports Nut

Dear Sports Nut,
If the TV is not too heavy, simply open your window and throw it out. This works best if you live in a high-rise apartment building. Make sure there are no pedestrians walking below.

Horrible Household Rule #2

Joint Ownership!

"What's yours is mine and what's mine is mine!"

It's important that your partner shares his/her possessions with you freely.

Leave his/her stuff carelessly around the house, just so she/he knows you're using it.

His/her CDs are your CDs, though your CDs should never be borrowed.

Intentionally break your partner's valuables to test his/her love and commitment to you and to get a peek at his/her dark side.

Sell his/her precious family heirlooms as a way of encouraging them to let go of the past.

Use his/her credit cards without asking permission to test his/her trust and to say, "I am in this relationship for better or worse."

```
Dear Doctor Dread,
My girlfriend is constantly nagging
me. She doesn't think we talk
enough. She blames me that I don't
share my feelings with her. What
can I do to get her off my back?
                         Yours truly,
                           Nagged


Dear Nagged,
Share with her how angry you feel
when she is constantly on your
back. Tell her that you "feel" she
is a nag. This will help her under-
stand your feelings.
```

Horrible Household Rule #3

Random Acts of Rudeness!

"Better to stab someone in the back than
in the front!"

From time to time, test your partner's commitment to you by practicing random acts of
rudeness.

Keep them off balance and show them that you
are not someone to be fooled with.

Project a not-so-subtle vibe of, "It's my way or
the highway."

It's best to surprise your partner when they are
least expecting it!

Just say stuff like "I don't trust you!," "Why are
you so uncaring?," "You are cheating on me!"

Try and target your partner's weak spots!

From time to time, ladies should cut their men down to size!

Guys should periodically make rude comments about their woman's weight and appearance.

It is much easier to be critical than to be correct.

BENJAMIN DISRAELI

Part 2

How to Get Fired!

Learn the "How to Get Fired!" techniques if

you want to leave your job quickly.

You probably have mastered some of these tips already but it is helpful to be reminded. Be persistent because some employers just won't fire you no matter what.

Provoking Fights at Work!

If you want to start a fight with someone in the workplace it's helpful to make accusations. Question the integrity, honesty, and work ethic of your opponent. Try and get your boss and coworkers to gang up on your adversary. Secretly observe your enemy to discover his/her weak spots!

Here are some subtle and not-so-subtle fight-provoking comments you can use in the workplace!

Use Against Adversary in a Group Setting:
"Why aren't you a team player?"
"Why do you resent us so much?"

Use When Alone with Adversary:
"Have you been gossiping about me?"
"Do you know why you're so unpopular?"

Use Against Adversary When Boss Is Close By:
"Are you surfing the internet again?"
"Did I hear you are looking for another job?"
"Were you late again?"

Bad Employee of the Month #1

Pathetic Punctuality

"Forget about being on time.
Live in the moment!"

Of course, you can just not show up for work and get fired.

But it is more fashionable to be late!

Plan your arrival about 30 minutes to 2 hours after your scheduled work time.

Lunch and coffee breaks are a good time to extend your absences from work.

Try and spend about half your workday away from the office doing your own personal errands.

Don't explain why you are late—excuses are for wimps.

Just tell all concerned that arriving fashionably late is your own personal style and will continue indefinitely.

Dear Doctor Dread,
My job sucks so bad I can't stand it another minute. I am going crazy, what should I do?
                              Yours truly,
                                Job Sucks

Dear Job Sucks,
You should not show up for work. Don't ever contact them again. Steal office equipment before you disappear. Make sure they can't keep your paycheck from you before you vanish!

Bad Employee of the Month #2

Professional Procrastinator

"The more you do, the more to do!"

Not accomplishing anything is an effective way to get fired.

Push all deadlines back!

Advertise the fact of your extreme inefficiency.

Be a cog in the corporate wheel!

Keep people chasing after you to turn in your work.

Be proud of your poor productivity—you have more important personal stuff to do!

Try and pass your workload to unsuspecting coworkers.

Just say it's not in your job description.

Tell your boss you just don't feel like getting anything done!

Strive to do the minimum required!

It's cool to be lazy.

Work is a necessary evil to be avoided.

MARK TWAIN

Better be wise by the misfortunes of others than by your own.

AESOP

Wise men don't need advice. Fools won't take it.

BENJAMIN FRANKLIN

Meeting Maniac

"A small thorn can cause an elephant tremendous pain!"

At meetings, try and waste everyone's time.

During a conference, talk often and for long periods of time.

Complain!

Point out lots of problems but offer no solutions!

Focus your mindless chatter on unrelated matters.

Be evasive and don't give a straight answer when asked a question.

Talk loudly and blame others at every opportunity.

Create an eerie vibe in the meeting room with sudden cries out loud or bursts of wailing laughter at other people's comments.

Wise men don't need advice. Fools won't take it.

BENJAMIN FRANKLIN

Bad Employee Of The Month #4

Just Say No!

"The eternal answer to all questions is 'No'!"

You will receive many requests while on the job.

Just say no before, during, and after requests are given to you.

Say no rudely and with force.

Make a facial expression that shows your contempt toward requesters.

Avoid all coworkers that may need something from you.

See how long you can flee without getting tracked down.

And if cornered with a request, "just say no"!

No, No, No, No, No, No!!!!

Or, of course, you can say yes but mean no!

Bad Employee of the Month #5

Junk E-mails!

"If message not received, then it never existed!"

If you need to return an e-mail, make sure you discuss everything but the mailer's requests.

Delete, Delete, Delete, Delete!!!

Feel the freedom!

Junk all e-mails!

After weeks of trashing e-mails, it may become tempting to read one from your boss. But if he won't talk to you in person then he doesn't deserve a response.

Your reply e-mail should be completely unrelated to the topic being discussed.

Forward your colleague's private e-mails to the whole company.

Denial ain't just a river in Egypt.
MARK TWAIN

Bad Employee of the Month #6

Client Cruelty!

"Good service, bad service—one and the same!"

The client is a company's most treasured possession and potentially your quickest route to getting fired.

If you are brutally careless with your clients, you are bound to get some complaints.

Unfortunately the client has become so accustomed to poor service that they are quite willing to tolerate a lot of crap.

It's good to really let your clients know that you have no interest in taking care of their needs.

Let them know that you resent their demands on your precious time!

Tell them they are the source of your entire life's misery.

Simply ignore them!

Avoid their calls, e-mails, and any other methods they may use to try to get your attention!

My father taught me to work; he did not teach me to love it.

ABRAHAM LINCOLN

Bad Employee of the Month #7

You Be the Boss!

"To lead or to follow—is your choice!"

Since your boss holds all your job security cards, spread rumors about him/her and make sure everyone knows the source.

Surf the internet whenever your boss drops by.

If your boss is heading towards you, talk loudly on your cell phone to friends and family.

Try to get caught sleeping under your desk. Or sit in your chair naked, working quietly.

```
Dear Doctor Dread,
My boss is constantly on my back
complaining I don't do enough.
What should I do?

                    Yours truly,
                    Bossy Boss

Dear Bossy Boss,
It's time for you to start tak-
ing control of your life! Start
parking your car in your boss's
parking spot. Make yourself at
home working from his desk.
Change the lock on his office
door. Just sit back in his chair
and smile until security breaks
down the door and throws you out
of the building.
```

Company Policy

1. Be Late!

2. Be Sloppy!

3. Be Rude!

4. Be Negative!

5. Be Lazy!

6. Be Selfish!

7. Be Dumb!

8. Be Blaming!

The fool doth think he is wise, but the wise man knows himself to be a fool.

WILLIAM SHAKESPEARE

Part 3

How to Get Depressed!

The goal of "How to Get Depressed!" is to help you feel really bad about yourself.

Maintain a dim outlook on life!

Stay focused on the idea that life is meaningless. Combat good moods with depressing mantras. You decide how you feel, so . . . stay focused on what a bummer life is. Watch the evening news to help you feel depressed on a global scale. Practice mind control by repeating over and over, "I hate my life!"

◎ ◎ ◎

13 Easy Ways to Stay Miserable!

Focus on these phrases to maintain a negative outlook on life!

Always think the worst of others!
Give up on life!
Be lazy!
Don't trust others!
Hate yourself!
Be rude!
Don't have fun!
Avoid exercise!
Don't change!
Repress your emotions!
Just stay in bed!

In three words I can sum up everything I've learned about life: it goes on.

ROBERT FROST

Miserable Tip #1

Be Your Own Personal Trainer!

Negative Affirmation (please repeat 5 times):

"I hate exercising!"

Exercise is the enemy of depression.

Avoid any activity that resembles a cardio workout.

Yoga and meditation should be avoided at all costs.

Inactivity will help you feel down!

It's best to try and not move your body much at all.

Flicking the remote control, walking to the fridge, and going to the bathroom are all

O.K. activities! But for the most part, try to stay motionless.

In time you will feel stagnant and completely unmotivated.

Dear Doctor Dread,
I feel so depressed! I can't make it another day. What should I do?
Yours truly,
Down & Out

Dear Down & Out,
Just stay in bed! Don't share with anyone how you are feeling. Isolate yourself in your own misery. Someday, in the distant future, you may or may not feel better. It's best to wait it out alone.

Phobias for You!!

Looking for some new and exciting things to avoid?

Amathophobia — Fear of dust

Decoraphobia — Fear of interior decorating

Heortophobia — Fear of holidays

Pogophobia — Fear of beards

Genuphobia — Fear of knees

Scopophobia — Fear of being naked

Chorophobia — Fear of dancing

Ospresiophobia — Fear of body odor

Odontophobia — Fear of teeth

Hodophobia — Fear of travel

Miserable Tip #2

Negative Support Buddies!

Negative Affirmation (please repeat 5 times):

"Life is hopeless!"

Have a support system in place to help you stay depressed.

Go for a coffee or talk on the phone with one of your negative support buddies.

Share with each other about the negative aspects of life.

Be victims together!

Find things to criticize about your friends.

Wallow in your depression.

Blame the world for your misfortunes!

Talk about how horrible you feel, moment by moment.

Try sitting silently miserable together!

Dear Doctor Dread,
I feel very happy and content lately. I am wondering if something is wrong with me. What do you think?

Yours truly,
Happyoholic

Dear Happyoholic,
Don't worry—the feeling will go away soon. Just stay focused on being miserable. Start instigating verbal confrontations with friends and family. Spend time contemplating what is rotten about your life.

Important Things to Avoid

Avoid any form of aerobic exercise, such as brisk walking, biking, or jogging!

Avoid playing your favorite music and dancing!

Avoid singing in the shower!

Avoid rolling down your car window and laughing out loud!

Avoid dogs, cats, or any other pets!

Avoid having plants and/or a garden!

Avoid uplifting movies!

Avoid inspiring books!

Avoid healthy food and sugar-free, non-caffeine beverages!

Miserable Tip #3

Negative Outlook on Life!

Negative Affirmation (please repeat 5 times):

"Life will always be hopeless!"

Look for opportunities to share your negative point of view.

Proudly insist on how much life sucks!

Do this whether you are rambling to yourself or actually having a conversation with someone.

When you speak, start your sentences with, "I hate" or "That sucks" or "It's all hopeless!" or "It won't work" or "Forget about it."

Maintaining a dim outlook on life takes practice!

```
Dear Doctor Dread,
I find it exhausting to have a
positive outlook on life. I am
tired of smiling all the time!
Can you give me some advice?
                    Yours truly,
              Positively Negative

Dear Positively Negative,
Stop trying to swim upstream.
Just go with the negative flow!
Drop your happy face and succumb
to your misery!
```

Celebrate the Holiday Blues

The holidays are the perfect time to be depressed and lonely, even if you have family and friends close by. The holiday blues will help you feel down, even if you are not prone to depression.

Here are some suggestions to help you increase seasonal anxiety:

Stay really busy to help create lots of stress and fatigue.

Remind yourself of your financial constraints.

Focus on how irritating your relatives are.

Commiserate with others about better holidays gone by.

Set unrealistic expectations for the season.

Don't keep lists and make random chaotic plans.

Don't volunteer time to help others in need.

Surround yourself with unsupportive people.

Absolutely don't take time for yourself!

Inside the Mind of a Depressed Person!

READ AT YOUR OWN RISK!

I feel horrible! My body feels like shit! I don't want to exercise! Life sucks! I am lonely! Nobody cares about me! I can't go another day! Life is boring! I hate everything! I just want to disappear into nothing! I can't go another second! Please someone shoot me! I feel so lazy! I don't want to do anything! I only want to veg out in front of the TV. I want to stuff my face until I puke! Life is torture! I am such a loser! Life is hell! I feel horrible! My body feels like shit! I don't want to exercise! Life sucks! I am lonely! Nobody cares about me! I can't go another day! Life is boring! I hate everything! I just want to melt into nothing! I can't go another second! Please someone shoot me! I feel so lazy! I don't want to do anything! I only want to veg out in front of the TV. I want to stuff my face until I puke! Life is torture! I am such a loser! Life is hell! I just want to melt into nothing! I can't go another second! Please someone shoot me! I feel so lazy! I don't want to do anything! I only want to veg out in front of the TV. I want to stuff my face until I puke! Life is torture! I am such a loser! Life is hell! Life is hell! Life is hell! I feel horrible! My body feels like shit! I don't want to exercise! Life sucks! I am lonely! Nobody cares about me! I can't go another day! Life is boring! I hate everything! I just want to melt into nothing! I can't go another second! Please someone shoot me! I feel so lazy! I don't want to do anything! I only want to veg out in front of the TV. I want to stuff my face until I puke! Life is torture! I am such a loser!

Part 4

How to Get Angry!

Anger is an important emotion to help you get through your day without anyone messing with you.

It's best to let things bother you!

Contemplate all the ways that you have been tricked and deceived in the past. Let people know just how much you resent them. Suppress your frustration until you have an outburst. Practice getting angry at others and at yourself!

◎ ◎ ◎

Anger Management Program #2

Right to Repress

"Treasure your resentments like old friends!"

The norm in society is to repress anger.

Each bump along the road of life gets stuffed down deep into our bellies.

In time, anger becomes a molten pool of lava boiling in our stomachs.

Keep a cap on your anger until it erupts like a volcano.

Play the "Who will erupt first" game!

Make rude pokes at each other and see who explodes first!

You can also practice this technique with strangers!

Anger Management Program #1

Unhealthy Releases

"Anger is a gift that keeps giving!"

The important thing is to choose how and where you let your anger out!

1. Strangers are a good target because you usually will never see them again.

2. You can enjoy anonymity if you dump your anger out while driving. It's helpful to have tinted windows!

3. Customer service people are required to take all the crap you can dish out. Unleash all the complaints you can muster and feel free to dump residual frustration on them.

4. Your loved ones are quite willing to absorb your anger. They often get angry back so you

can maintain a healthy war of words on a daily basis. In time you will loose track of who is at fault and you can just fight for the sake of fighting.

How much more grievous are the
consequences of anger than
the causes of it.

MARCUS AURELIUS

Speak when you are angry
and you will make the
best speech you will ever regret.

AMBROSE BIERCE

Do not use a hatchet to remove a fly from your
friend's forehead.

CHINESE PROVERB

Anger Management Program #3

Pass the Blame

"Give generously to others, especially your anger!"

Pass the blame!

If you feel angry, look for someone to blame it on.

If you feel threatened or vulnerable, just get angry.

Roar out loud! This is the best way to release your frustration

Feel sad? Get mad!

Feel hurt? Get horrible!

Fortunately most people deal with anger in the same way. So we can fuel each other's rage.

One small disturbance can turn into a battle!

Anger Management Program #4

Recreational Road Rage

"Irritation is the spice of life!"

Driving through rush hour traffic can be a thrill.

Try and irritate the drivers around you.

Honk your horn often for no apparent reason.

Tailgate the car in front of you.

See how close you can maneuver your car without making contact with the car next to you.

Driving is an opportunity to let out your inner evil villain!

Use your imagination!

Chat aggressively with the drivers around you.

Think up mean names for the people driving in front and behind you!

Use your drive time efficiently; contemplate all the things that irritate you in life. Then let it out on the drivers around you!

Experience is a dear teacher, and only fools will learn from no other.

BENJAMIN FRANKLIN

Anger Management Program #5

Waiting Warrior

"Life is like one endless line!"

It's important to focus on how irritating it is to wait.

Make rude gestures to those waiting in line with you.

It is helpful to carry heavy bags while you wait in line in order to create a strain on your neck and back and make you extra grouchy.

When it is finally your turn, do your business in super slow motion.

Feel the energetic daggers flying your way from the customers waiting behind you.

Anger Management Program #6

Break Stuff

"Temporary insanity is only temporary!"

If you really feel frustrated, try kicking a hard object.

Or punch something.

These techniques tend to be quite painful.

You may break a bone but you might also get some temporary anger relief.

The harder you punch or kick, the more anger will be released.

It is especially effective to break things.

Valuable possessions are often the best targets.

Break your own things if you are mad at yourself.

If you are angry with someone else, then break his/her stuff.

No great genius has ever existed
without some touch of madness.

ARISTOTLE

Top 10 Outrageous Anger Outlets

1. Tackle strangers in the street!

2. Pick a fight with someone bigger than you!

3. Punch and kick solid objects!

4. Swear obscenities in public!

5. Scream at people!

6. Start arguments with family and friends!

7. Write ridiculous complaints to corporations!

8. Be mean to customer service people!

9. Aggressively honk your horn while driving!

10. Get mad at politicians!

If you are patient in one moment
of anger, you will escape a hundred days
of sorrow.

CHINESE PROVERB

Anger Management Program #7

Embrace Your Anger!

*"To succeed on your journey,
you must step on many toes!"*

Anger will give you an edge over the competition.

Always be ready to defend yourself!

Enjoy the rush of chemicals that release into your bloodstream as you prepare for battle.

Get pumped up as your breathing begins to increase and blood is detoured to your muscles for extra strength.

Flex!

Enjoy the high as your rational mind disengages and your thoughts become distorted.

You are a mean fighting machine, engaged and ready for a war!

Extra Anger Benefits: weakened immune system, bowel irritation, ulcers, heart attacks, strokes, and high blood pressure!

Life's tragedy is that we get old too soon and wise too late.

BENJAMIN FRANKLIN

Holding on to anger is like grasping a hot coal with the intent of throwing it at someone else; you are the one who gets burned.

BUDDHA

10 Miserable Mental Mantras

Focus on these phrases to help you feel pissed off throughout your day!

1. People are stupid!

2. Electronic devices are too confusing!

3. I have too much work to do!

4. Family and friends are irritating!

5. Long lines suck!

6. The roads are full of rotten drivers!

7. Everyone wants something from me!

8. Life is all work!

9. Things never go as planned!

10. I'm always late!

Inside the Mind of an Angry Person!

PLEASE READ AT YOUR OWN RISK!

I want to spread my anger to everyone I meet. When I feel angry, I want to hurt other people. I look for people who I can hate. It doesn't take much; in fact, it doesn't really matter what people do. If I am really pissed off, I can make shit up. Stupid people and stupid situations are the cause of my anger. I am a victim of a stupid world. I love to get cut off by another car because then I can honk my horn and scream at the stupid driver. When a customer service person is rude to me, I let out my anger freely. When my spouse says something I don't like, I let out my anger. When I see something on TV that frustrates me, I let out my anger. When my neighbor irritates me, I let out my anger. When I see my credit card bill I get angry. When I have too much coffee, cigarettes, or alcohol, I get even angrier. Angry, Angry, Angry, Angry, Angry, Angry, Angry, Angry!!! I want to spread my anger to everyone I meet. When I feel angry, I want to hurt other people. I look for people who I can hate. It doesn't take much; in fact, it doesn't really matter what people do. If I am really pissed off, I can make shit up. Stupid people and stupid situations are the cause of my anger. I am a victim of a stupid world. I love to get cut off by another car because then I can honk my horn and scream at the stupid driver. When a customer service person is rude to me, I let out my anger freely. When I see something on TV that frustrates me, I let out my anger. When my neighbor irritates me, I let out my anger.

How to Get Stressed!

To reach and maintain higher levels of stress and overwhelm, you need to practice using these tools.

Worry is a wonderful stress tool.

Multitasking is very helpful in promoting anxiety. Taking on more than you can handle gets you stressed in no time. Conflict with others is a fabulous way to remain tense. Financial problems can take you to new levels of worry and hopelessness. Being really stressed is an easy state to live in. It eventually becomes addictive.

Stress Management Workbook

This program will encourage you to think stressful thoughts and increase your overwhelm!

List the many things that stress you out.
(Practice them regularly.)

Write down everything that is wrong in your life.
(Think about those things as often as possible.)

List everything that could go wrong in your life.
(Think about why you deserve it.)

List the many ways that others have done you wrong.
(Contemplate ways you can have revenge.)

Write down all your faults.
(Feel hopeless about yourself.)

Insane Stress Tool #1

Weight of the World on Your Shoulders!

"To make dreams reality, worry about them!"

Feel the weight of the world on your shoulders!

Just imagine it's you against the world!

Feel your body slumping down as you make your way through the day.

Keep your neck and shoulders tight.

As your shoulders climb up towards your ears, try and keep them there permanently. Imagine your shoulders are glued to your ears.

Dear Doctor Dread,
I have many urgent deadlines
coming up! I keep trusting that
everything will be O.K. and that
I can get the help I need to
complete my tasks. Do you have
any advice for me during these
busy times?

Yours Truly,
Merrily Multitasking

Dear Merrily Multitasking,
You are in denial! Don't pull on
your coworkers. They will get all
the glory. Do everything on your
own. Stay up late at night and
drink lots of coffee. Suck it up.
That's what work is for . . . to
get stressed out!

Stress Side Effects!

These are the side effects that you can look forward to from stress!

Mood swings

Fatigue

Headaches

Anxiety

Poor concentration

Loss of appetite

Ulcers

Overwhelm

Impatience

Anger

Depression

Frustration

Bad decisions

Life is really simple, but we insist on making it complicated.

CONFUCIUS

Insane Stress Tool #2

Multitasking on the Move

"A person who runs behind a car gets exhausted."

Driving in your car is a fabulous time to get stressed.

While you drive, try to do as many things as possible.

Drinking coffee or other hot beverages is especially effective. You can spill it and burn yourself while you drive.

Try shaving or putting on lipstick at stoplights.

Rush hour is the best time to multitask: the stop and go traffic can make you crazy!

You can literally put your life in danger just trying to dial your cell phone while driving in busy traffic!

Quick Stress Tips
On the Go!

These three programs will help you stay tense wherever you are!

Shallow Breathing Meditation

Shallow breathing is convenient because you can practice it anywhere and any time you feel relaxation creeping in. Take short, constrained breaths! Quickly draw the air in and out of your lungs. Imagine you are hyperventilating! Practice this technique to stay tense.

Tense Muscle Technique

Find a crowded, noisy place. Focus on tensing all your muscles from your head to your toes at the same time. If you feel your muscles begin to relax, tense them up again. Concentrate on worry and overwhelm.

Negative Imagery

Think of a horrible, depressing time in your life and recreate the experience. Close your eyes and imagine yourself in that tense, chaotic situation that made you so unhappy. See, feel, smell, taste, and touch the nightmarish experience. Notice how gloomy everything becomes!

When angry, count to four; when very angry, swear.

MARK TWAIN

The difference between genius and stupidity is that genius has its limits.

ALBERT EINSTEIN

When we remember we are all mad, the mysteries disappear and life stands explained.

MARK TWAIN

Insane Stress Tool #3

Overwhelm for Couch Potatoes

"First there was thought, then stress!"

You don't have to be busy to be stressed.

Practice negative mind control.

Focus on the many tasks you are doing.

What problems and challenges do you face?

If you worry enough, you can practically have an anxiety attack just chillin' on the sofa. Keep depressing shows playing on the TV for negative mind programming.

The evening news is always helpful to remind you of how miserable life can be.

Dear Doctor Dread,
Lately I feel at peace within myself! I live a life of leisure. I exercise, eat well, don't work much, and get a massage every week! Do you think my stressful times are behind me?

Yours Truly,
At Peace

Dear At Peace,
You should take up some stressful hobbies! Call 800 numbers and wait on hold for long periods of time. Build something without reading the instruction manual. Go for a drive in rush-hour traffic. In no time, your peaceful state will vanish and you will feel stressed out once again!

Insane Stress Program #4
Fiendish Feng Shui

"Scattered possessions, scattered thoughts!"

It's important to remain disorganized!

Pile your stuff as high as possible and keep your space permanently cluttered. This helps crush the flow of creative "chi" energy.

You want your work and living space to become stagnant and dead like a swamp.

If you pile things high enough, no one can get close enough to bother you.

Become literally lost in an ocean of misplaced items!

Try this on-the-job exercise:

Fiendishly Feng Shui your coworker's work-space! Take all his/her files out, close your eyes, take a deep relaxing breath, and throw every-thing up into the air. Quietly sneak out of his/her office.

For every minute you remain angry, you give up sixty seconds of peace of mind.

RALPH WALDO EMERSON

Let's All Get Stressed Together!!!

75–90% of visits to primary care physicians are for stress-related disorders or complaints.

Over 90% of disease is caused or complicated by stress.

Americans spend over $11 billion per year trying to cope with stress.

The secret to humor is surprise.

ARISTOTLE

Top 13 Tips for Overwhelm

This program will assist you to always remain stressed no matter what you are doing!

1. Lie and cheat!

2. Be dishonest and feel guilty!

3. Work long hours every day!

4. Try and remember everything in your head!

5. Never take a break!

6. Do everything at once!

7. Handle it all alone!

8. Choose rush hour to go places!

9. Leave important tasks to the last minute!

10. Go into debt!

11. Create unrealistic deadlines!

12. Make an impossible to-do list!

13. Tell yourself it's never enough!

Insane Stress Program #5

Anxiety Attack Technique!

"You must focus on frustration!"

Find a bench near a busy intersection or other hectic place.

Sit anxiously in an uncomfortable position for a long period of time.

Review in your mind all the things you should worry about.

Repeat your stress mantra, "I am stressed, I am stressed."

Don't breathe.

Tense your muscles for as long as possible.

Look around in a frantic way.

Have a cigarette and puff quickly.

Six Easy Steps for Stressful Shopping

If you are feeling down, jump in your car and head for the mall!

Take a break from your hectic life and go shopping! Just charge it! With each purchase, feel all your stress and worries building.

1. Don't forget to bring all your credit cards.
2. Look for items that you don't need and that can't be returned!
3. Follow the latest trends. Then there will be something new to buy every season.
4. Buy stuff without looking at the price tag!
5. Randomly put things in your cart and buy them for the sake of buying.
6. Keep purchasing items until either you max out your credit cards or max out the carry space in your car.

If you are a coach potato and too lazy to take a drive, just turn the TV on to the home shopping channel and start purchasing. The internet is also great for random shopping sprees.

Insane Stress Program #6

Random Day Planner

"Forget your appointments; forget your worries!"

Make sure you leave your possessions strewn about in a random manner. This way, when you are late for an appointment and need your car keys, you can double your overwhelm trying to figure out where your keys are.

Enlightened to-do list:
Help save the forests by not writing your daily activities down. Busy days are the best time to try and remember everything in your head. Just be in the moment and let yourself forget important appointments. If you don't accomplish what you need to do, then it wasn't meant to be.

Inside the Mind of a Stressed Person!

PLEASE READ AT YOUR OWN RISK!

I have so much to do! I'll never get everything done! It's hopeless! I am broke! It will never work! This project is messed up! I'm late! I can't remember everything that I have to do! Everything is a mess! I can't figure this out! I'm late! I have so much to do! I'll never get everything done! It's hopeless! I am broke! It will never work! This project is messed up! I'm late! I can't remember everything that I have to do! Everything is a mess! I can't figure this out! I'm late! I have so much to do! I'll never get everything done! It's hopeless! I am broke! It will never work! This project is messed up! I'm late! I can't remember everything that I have to do! Everything is a mess! I can't figure this out! I'm late! I have so much to do! I'll never get everything done! It's hopeless! I am broke! It will never work! This project is messed up! I'm late! I can't remember everything that I have to do! Everything is a mess! I can't figure this out! I'm late! I have so much to do! I'll never get everything done! It's hopeless! I am broke! It will never work! This project is messed up! I'm late! I can't remember everything that I have to do! Everything is a mess! I can't figure this out! I'm late! I have so much to do! I'll never get everything done! It's hopeless! I am broke! It will never work! This project is messed up! I'm late! I can't remember everything that I have to do! Everything is a mess! I can't figure this out! I'm late! I have so much to do! I'll never get everything done! It's hopeless! I am broke! It will never work! This project is messed up!

In this world nothing is certain but death and taxes.

BENJAMIN FRANKLIN

HAPPILY EVER AFTER!

Hopefully you had some good laughs while you read this book!

Don't worry if you kept thinking "I do that."

We all do!

The point of this book is not to get lost in the hopeless-ness of life but to shed light on the many self-destructive habits we all have!

By seeing the problem you are halfway to the solution.

So keep on your merry way and don't be hard on yourself if you stumble and start messing your life up!

It's best to simply realize your mistakes, be humbled, apologize to innocent bystanders, and be grateful you are becoming more aware of yourself and the world you live in!

Take care, and I hope to bump into you on planet Earth someday!

DARRIN ZEER

ACKNOWLEDGMENTS

Special thanks to Damien's home cookin' and my editing angels Alison and Daisy.

Thanks to all the gang at Red Wheel/Weiser, in particular my editors Mike Conlon, Brenda Knight, and Caroline Pincus.

Thanks to my friends for their many helpful tips on *How to Mess Up Your Life!* Franz, Hans, Chiara, Patria, Berek, Oliver, Kiersten, Elizabeth, Gwen, Gina, Chelsea, Trinity, and everyone else.

ABOUT THE AUTHOR

While Darrin stays pretty busy messing up his life,
he also is the author of several books, including
the best-selling *Office Yoga*. He spent seven years
traveling throughout Asia studying various forms
of yoga and meditation. He has appeared on CNN,
as well as in *Time* magazine, the *Wall Street Journal*
and the *New York Times*. He currently lives in San
Diego, California.

If you would like to share your own special tips
and tricks on how to mess up your life, feel free to
contact Darrin at: *www.howtomessupyourlife.com*

TO OUR READERS

Conari Press, an imprint of Red Wheel/Weiser, publishes books on topics ranging from spirituality, personal growth, and relationships to women's issues, parenting, and social issues. Our mission is to publish quality books that will make a difference in people's lives—how we feel about ourselves and how we relate to one another. We value integrity, compassion, and receptivity, both in the books we publish and in the way we do business.

Our readers are our most important resource, and we value your input, suggestions, and ideas about what you would like to see published. Please feel free to contact us, to request our latest book catalog, or to be added to our mailing list.

Conari Press
An imprint of Red Wheel/Weiser
500 Third Street, Suite 230
San Francisco, CA 94107
www.redwheelweiser.com